Test your

Numeracy

GARETH LEWIS

Series editors: GARETH LEWIS & GENE CROZIER

Hodder & Stoughton

A MEMBER OF THE HODDER HEADLINE GROUP

Orders: please contact Bookpoint Ltd, 39 Milton Park, Abingdon, Oxon OX14 4TD. Telephone: (44) 01235 400414, Fax: (44) 01235 400454. Lines are open from 9.00 – 6.00, Monday to Saturday, with a 24 hour message answering service. Email address: orders@bookpoint.co.uk

British Library Cataloguing in Publication Data
A catalogue record for this title is available from The British Library

ISBN 0 340 78289 7

First published 2000
Impression number   10 9 8 7 6 5 4 3 2 1
Year   2004 2003 2002 2001 2000

Typeset by Fakenham Photosetting Limited, Fakenham, Norfolk.
Printed in Great Britain for Hodder & Stoughton Education, a division of Hodder Headline Plc, 338 Euston Road, London NW1 3BH by Cox & Wyman Ltd, Reading, Berkshire.

in *the Institute*
of Management

The Institute of Management (IM) is the leading
organisation for professional management. Its purpose is
to promote the art and science of management in every
sector and at every level, through research, education,
training and development, and representation of
members' views on management issues.

This series is commissioned by IM Enterprises Limited,
a subsidiary of the Institute of Management, providing
commercial services.

**Management House,
Cottingham Road,
Corby,
Northants NN17 1TT
Tel: 01536 204222;
Fax: 01536 201651
Website: http://www.inst-mgt.org.uk**

Registered in England no 3834492
Registered office: 2 Savoy Court, Strand,
London WC2R 0EZ

Contents

Introduction

Numeracy is important to all of us. It is important in terms of how well we can cope with many aspects of our normal life – from managing our finances to going on holiday. Perhaps more importantly, for people with responsible jobs or management roles, it is also vital in our working life.

In a world increasingly dominated by information, and where much of that information is in digital or numerical form, we need as professionals to be able to master the basic mathematical operations, and to feel comfortable and confident in our numerical skills.

Yet it is a sad fact that so many of us don't feel this way. For a complex variety of reasons, some related to our early experiences at school, many of us do not feel we have the competence and skill we need to cope with the mathematics of everyday working life.

Against this background, numeracy, and numerical reasoning form a part of many testing and assessment processes used by organisations for anything from recruitment through to development, and selection for progression. It is no wonder that this can cause anxiety for many.

This book is for those people who want to know more about some of the following:

- What are the important skills I need
- How are they assessed
- How good are my skills (or not)
- What I can do about it

The book, then, will explain the range of numerical skills used at work and their applications, as well as how to develop some of those skills. As with all of the books in the 'Test Yourself' series, we give you the opportunity to assess and evaluate your own range of skills, so that you will know much better where you stand.

The book is arranged in the following sections:

- The importance of numeracy
- Aspects of numeracy
- How numeracy is tested
- Test your numeracy
- Developing your skills

The importance of numeracy

In this first chapter we shall consider why numeracy is important to so many people, particularly in their working lives. To do that we shall look at:

* Numeracy in the world
* Numeracy at work
* The needs of the individual

Numeracy in the world

A simple fact of life is this:

Mathematics matters ...

Mathematics is one of the primary ways in which we deal with the external world of realities, and has been for thousands of years. In fact, it has been argued that mathematical ability is programmed into our brains genetically, as part of our way of coping with the world around us. The earliest human beings needed spatial and geometrical awareness to navigate in their environment. They needed to be able to judge distances, angles and positions to move around in the trees. They needed to be able to judge the size of predator animals to evaluate risk and threat.

Similarly, they needed to be able to judge distances and time to be able to travel distances and return. They needed to be able to count in order to assess the threat from groups of hostile animals or rivals. And with the keeping of animals and basic barter, they needed to be able to manipulate numbers.

Since the time of ancient civilizations, people have used the basic ideas and concepts of mathematics as a way of processing, classifying, ordering and understanding the world around them. In the first instance, this was done by noticing patterns in the movements of the stars and the planets in the sky. The notions of trade and currency are impossible without basic arithmetic skills. And the ability to build dwellings, palaces and holy buildings is only possible with the development and use of sophisticated means of measuring distances and quantities.

Think of the complicated arithmetic and geometry that was necessary to build the ancient pyramids. In ancient civilizations on the Indian subcontinent, there were complicated rules to define distance and proportions in the building of holy places.

What was true then is equally true for the world of today. We need mathematical skills to interpret not only what goes on in the world around us, but also to be able to cope and play a full part in our society.

Just think of the following:

- Going shopping
- Going on holiday
- Managing a bank account
- Buying a house and starting a mortgage
- Decorating or doing DIY
- Planning and undertaking a journey
- Using a recipe to cook a meal for a family or a group of people
- Running an amateur sports club

None of these could be accomplished without a confident grasp of some basic mathematical or arithmetical ideas.

Numeracy at work

If maths and arithmetic are such a vital and integral part of our everyday world, it is not surprising that they also feature strongly in almost all aspects of the world of work.

'Mention the word 'maths' and many people start to panic. People will do almost anything to avoid a sum. And, all too often, people seem almost proud of being hopeless with numbers. Unlike reading, people will readily admit that they can't do maths – as if it doesn't matter.

But it does matter. We all need a feel for numbers. Imagine how difficult life would be if we did not have the ability to deal with numbers – coping with mortgages, pensions, credit card bills or time zones. Even simple shopping becomes a nightmare.

And most jobs require basic numeracy skills. In fact, poor numeracy has been shown to be more of a problem than poor literacy in staying in full time employment.

Conversely, maths qualifications have been linked to success in the workplace – graduates with a maths 'A' level were found to earn 10% more than other graduates when they started work.' (From the Mathsyear 2000 website.)

So many people in the world of work need to be interested in numeracy. But that interest is a complex thing, comprising many facets for different people. Here are a few different perspectives:

1. 25-year old graduate in their first job in sales and
   marketing
   *'My first degree was in media studies. I haven't done any
   maths since year 11, and I was no good at it then. Now I am
   expected to analyse data and make decisions ...'*
2. 35-year old property manager
   *'We are just doing some systematic psychometric testing and
   assessment in our organisation and I am terrified that my
   basic numeracy will let me down ...*
3. 45-year old senior manager in a travel company
   *'I have been afraid of maths all my life. I have managed to get
   away with hiding it, but now I want to get more confident for
   my own peace of mind. I feel stupid not being able to do the
   most basic of things with numbers. I am responsible for 12
   people and a large budget ...'*
4. Production team leader in a pharmaceutical company
   *'The job is becoming more information based. Such a lot of our
   work now is based on software and the intranet. I need skills to
   analyse and manage the information, that I just don't really
   have.'*

When you look at jobs in more detail, every aspect seems
to involve figures, quantitative information, and by
implication, arithmetic. Consider these examples:

Sales
A sales manager needs to make predictions about the sales
for his or her unit, and break this down into sales targets for
each of his/her sales staff. He needs to break the sales down
into the various product groups. He needs to know the
revenue that will result from these sales. He needs to know
the allocated resources, and what categories he will spend it
on (a budget). He also needs to monitor the actual figures

against these forecasts, and the actual spending on cars, equipment, travel and subsistence and so on.

Human resources
Someone in human resources might need a systematic way to allocate and monitor the use of the training rooms in their organisation. They need to know how many staff have been trained, and at what cost. They need to collect statistics about opinions on the value of the training to evaluate it. It is necessary to work out the costs of recruiting staff, and so on.

A nurse
One of the key skills for a nurse is to be able to work with measurements very accurately. Imagine the consequences if a nurse gets the volume of a drug wrong by a factor of 10! Similarly she/he has to be able to understand concentrations (the proportion of a substance in a liquid for example).

A manager in a call centre
As a manager in a banking call centre, it is important to keep track of a whole range of figures and statistics. How many calls do we predict in each hour, on each day for the coming week. How many hours each member of staff works. How many calls each member of staff takes in an hour, a day, and so on. What is the average duration of a call for each member of staff? How many calls are converted to sales? What are our total sales on a daily, weekly and monthly basis, and how are we doing compared to our predictions? A whole range of statistics need to be collected and compiled for us to know how well we are doing.

A cook in a school kitchen
We need to estimate the quantities of food to be ordered for the menus for each day, and week. We need to estimate the amount of food to prepare for the expected number of children who eat the school dinners. We need to keep a record of the expenditure on the food, and on the income from dinner money.

Most of these people will have been recruited for other technical and personal skills, but they require skills in mathematics and arithmetic to be able to cope and fulfil their job roles properly.

The changing world of work

The world of work is also changing. Nobody can have failed to notice the increasing use of computers in the world of work, or the impact that the internet is having on many organisations and jobs. The proportion of jobs in the service economy is growing compared to those in basic manufacturing. Many of these organisations, and the jobs within them are focused on information and knowledge, as this becomes a key aspect of the economy. The knowledge economy changes the requirements on us in terms of the skills we need to cope and flourish in this environment. So much more of the work is concerned with the processing of data, and much more of that data is in digital or quantitative form. These information processing skills are rooted in mathematics.

It is no exaggeration to say that all 'white collar' jobs, and any jobs that involve management or senior technical or functional specialism will require a level of mathematical or arithmetical ability. And these rquirements are growing and becoming more important.

We can sum this up by saying that if we genuinely live in an information age, where knowledge is the primary currency of the economy, then we can only manage that by developing and using our thinking skills. The ability to think is one of our primary skill sets. Within that, because of the proliferation of information in numerical and quantitative form, numeracy must be an important part of that repertoire of skills.

The personal perspective

At the end of the day, it is us as individuals that have to cope with the situations described above. Therefore, it is important to consider the human and personal impact of these changes and requirements. Here are a few aspects that should be considered.

Mathophobia

There is no doubt that the level of skills in the workforce as a whole is not as high as we would like it to be. This has been confirmed by much research and in numerous reports by many of the bodies interested in UK plc, over the years. Here are a few examples:

- 59% of organisations say basic numeracy skills are lacking in young people (IM survey, quoted in press release, Aug 1997)
- Only one in five Britons answered 12 basic numeracy questions correctly in a test
- 22% scored five or fewer correct answers

- British 16–24 year-olds performed worse than all other compatriot groups (including France, Holland, Japan, Sweden, Australia and Denmark) (Survey of people aged 16–60, Adult Basic Skills Agency, 1996)
- One in four people of a group of 1700 adults studied had 'very low numeracy skills' which made it hard to complete everyday tasks. (Research at City University, London)

Rarely a year goes by without some report in the newspapers lamenting the lack of numeracy skills in school leavers entering employment. That is the view, if you like, of employers or of the nation in general.

Citizenship and personal satisfaction
For all of the reasons set out above, most of us need a competent and confident level of numeracy skills to cope with and to thrive in the world in general, and particularly in the world of work.

However, there is another side to the story. This so-called lack of skills also has a human side. From the point of view of the individuals involved, this situation is also far from ideal. Again, there is a great deal of research that has shown that many adults are only too well aware of their shortcomings when it comes to numeracy and mathematics.

You could almost say it is the great hidden problem of the world of work. One reason we call this a hidden problem is because people who lack confidence or competence in numeracy tend to hide it and not talk about it.

Lack of competence or skill in other areas seems to be socially acceptable. How many people have you heard tell proudly that they don't know how to switch on a computer or program a video recorder? They do not admit so readily to being poor at basic arithmetic.

For many of these, it is not just a question of being poor at these basic skills. It is also a fact that they are afraid (hence the term 'mathophobia' – a fear of mathematics). Thus, they spend their lifetime – particularly their working lifetime, avoiding the need to do any arithmetic at all. They also cover up their inability because it is deemed socially unacceptable to admit to this. The one thing it is socially ok to admit is that:

'I hated mathematics at school.'

A lot of adults, many of them in quite senior positions and in jobs with substantial responsibility, have spent a lifetime developing strategies not only avoiding the need to do any mathematics, but also developing very intricate and sophisticated routines to avoid being found out and having to admit it.

There are of course, some notable exceptions to this. Adam Singer, a dyslexic who left school at 16 with just one O-level, now heads the £11bn rated company formed by the merger of Telewest and Flextech. Interviewed recently in the business section of a Sunday newspaper, he said:

'I can't add up to save my life.'

Perhaps there is hope for the rest of us yet!

There is a final consideration about why numeracy can be important to many people. And in the long term, this might be the most important reason of all in terms of motivation. It is the notion of self-satisfaction.

Many of those people we have referred to in the previous sections:

- Those who are mathophobic
- Those who hide their lack of numerical skill
- Those who would just like to be better or more confident at some of the more important numerical process

For all of these, it is not just the skill itself that is important, but something more personal. This has something to do with self confidence and being able to go about the world without being intimidated.

The testing and assessment environment

One reason that prompts many people to look, perhaps reluctantly, at their own ability and achievement in numeracy comes from career considerations.

Many people, when they are seeking to progress their career, know that to succeed at job applications often involves a component of psychometric testing. That in turn will often involve the testing of some aspects of numerical aptitude, ability or reasoning.

For others, assessment processes within their own organisation – whether for progression or for development purposes – may involve some aspects of testing of aptitude and ability, which in turn may have a numerical component. To some, this may fill them with dread. For most, they feel vulnerable and wish they had listened more closely when they were at school.

For all of these people, and for all of these reasons, this book is writen to help you to:

- Get an idea of your own level of skill and attainment
- Help you to develop confidence and competence in the major skill areas
- Describe the important aspects of numeracy, and how they are used in work, and how they are tested

Summary

In this chapter, we have seen that mathematics is important to the way we interpret and deal with the world. We have also shown that mathematics, and particularly basic numeracy, is vital for most people in being able to fulfil their job requirements confidently and successfully. Not only this, but in the new world economy of information and knowledge, computers and the internet, the processing of quantitative data, and all of the skills that go with it, are becoming ever more important.

Against this backdrop, we have outlined the 'hidden problem' of mathophobia and the lack of basic skills in numeracy that seems to exist in the workforce. For some people, this gets exposed only when they are subject to testing in their organisations.

This then, provides the business case for looking more closely at developing our numeracy skills. However, none of us can solve the problems of the economy single-handedly, but we can look to ourselves. The individual business case suggests that we should try to identify where we are, and more importantly, what we can do to develop our own skills.

This not only helps to satisfy the requirements at work, but also helps to build our own personal confidence and sense of satisfaction and achievement at work.

Aspects of numeracy

In this chapter we shall look at the various aspects and operations of numeracy that we need to get by in the world of work. We will do this by looking at:

- The scope of numeracy
- The basic skills
- Applications

The scope of numeracy

A good way of getting some ideas on the scope of numeracy is to look at it from a less usual perspective, and try our hands at a puzzle.

1 1 2 3 5 8 13 21

Do you notice anything about this sequence of numbers? Take your time.

If you can't figure out the sequence, apply a strategy that any mathematician would try and look at the differences between the successive terms (numbers in the sequence), to see if they tell you anything.

You may have noticed that the differences between each term (apart from the first difference) are the same numbers as the sequence itself, that is:

1 1 2 3 5 ...

So you can always get the next term, because you now know what the next difference is. If we turn this explanation around backwards, you can probably see that you can get each term of the sequence by adding the two previous ones together. Such sequences are called Fibannaci sequences after the Italian mathematician that discovered them.

Here is another one:

10	12	22	34	56	90

The two starting numbers are 10 and 12, and the sixth term is 90. Now, here's the challenge – choose two starting numbers so that the sixth term is exactly 100.

?	?				100

If you have done that – well done! You may have noticed that the mathematical skills (as you normally think of them) that you used are very, very simple. In fact, all you need to do is to be able to add up and take away. However, you also needed a whole range of other skills to be able to 'solve' this puzzle. These are what we call **process** skills. They involve guessing, checking, sorting, comparing, reasoning, and other general problem solving skills.

Of course, if you are a mathematician, you will be used to using some of these skills in a practised and disciplined way. Checking the differences, is a good example of a learnt strategy that you know is worth a try – even if you can't be sure it will give you the answer. If you were a mathematician you would also be likely to go on from here by asking a few questions, like:

- Are there any other pairs of numbers that lead to 100?
- How many pairs?
- Can I prove that these are the only pairs that lead to 100?
- Is there any pattern of the numbers of starting pairs that lead to a given 6th number?

And so on.

The point of this is that this puzzle is very like the way that numeracy is used in working environments.

In most working environments, the arithmetic is actually very simple. It is the reasoning applied to numbers that is the real skill. Most people have, and can further develop such reasoning skills, with a bit of practice. However, it is their fear of the arithmetic that puts them off 'flexing their muscles' with real numbers in working contexts. We should bear this in mind as we look at the aspects of numeracy of most interest to most people in their normal work.

Our ability to reason with numbers, and to use some of these higher level processes is related to our numerical aptitude and reasoning ability. We shall look at the way that this is assessed in the next chapter.

In this chapter, we shall look at the raw material (numbers), and those basic and very simple operations that account for most of what we need to do. You may well be surprised at how few simple operations we need to learn to master the numeracy required in most working environments.

The Pareto effect of learning
You may have noticed that there is a 'diminishing returns' effect in learning. Take the situation of learning something new like wordprocessing software. The first 80% of the functionality of the wordprocessor is easy to learn, and is learnt very quickly. It is learnt in something like 20% of the time, and accounts for perhaps 80% of the usage. The next 20% of the functionality takes 80% of the time and effort, and will only account for 20% of the usage.

This 80:20 effect is called the Pareto principle, after the Italian economist who discovered it. It accounts for many effects that we see in the real world (you can see how we use this effect in a later chapter).

What we are presenting here is the 20% of the knowledge that should account for 80% of the need for most people. It goes without saying that it only takes 20% of the time to learn. So the following is the quick and easy bit that accounts for the bulk of what most people need to know and to do in the working context. If, by chance, you need the extra, more specialised parts, you can much more easily follow up at a later date with some of the excellent specialised publications.

In most working contexts, it may seem surprising, but a small and limited number of operations account for the vast majority of processing that goes on. We shall cover them here.

The basic skills

Before we can perform any operations, we have to have objects to perform those operations on. In our case, that is numbers. So far that will be obvious, but of course, numbers can be sophisticated things.

The basic set of numbers is the counting numbers:

1 2 3 4 5 ...

By far the vast majority of operations we will be interested in will be done on this set of numbers. However, we can extend this set of numbers in a number of ways.

Firstly, we can count them backwards as well as forwards, and from 'the other side of zero' we get the negative numbers:

−5 −4 −3 −2 −1 0 1 ...

The total set is now called the integers. They are incredibly useful for showing negative quantities (or amounts owed, if you like). Modern accounting systems would not work without the ability to show negative numbers (although they tend to be shown like this (250) rather than like this −250)

The next way to extend the set of numbers is to put numbers between the integers. We can do this using fractions, or by using decimal intervals:

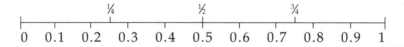

These latter prove to be very useful, for instance, in recording measurements of all kinds, and in representing and calculating amounts of money.

There are some other ways to extend the family of numbers, but on the whole, they tend to be specialised, and of interest mainly to mathematicians. Now we have our 'raw material', we can start to do things with it.

By far the most important processes we apply to numbers are the four basic operations of number, sometimes called the four rules:

- Addition
- Subtraction
- Multiplication
- Division

These are the basis for most applications, and if you can apply them to the set of whole numbers, together with decimal numbers, there is not much you can't do. In the final chapter, there is plenty of advice and practice on how to increase your confidence and facility with these basic operations.

At this stage it will be useful to get an accurate idea of how well you can use the basic operations with different aspects of number. We call this **numerical attainment**, and it represents how well you have learnt these things at school or since.

For each of these tests, you can use pencil and paper, but obviously not a calculator. When you have completed them, you can check the answers in the back of the book. The tests should give you a very detailed idea of which of these operations you can use accurately and fluently, and which you need to work on.

? Test Yourself

Quick Test 1 – the four rules with whole numbers
(answers on page 75)

1 9 + 15 **2** 27 + 16 **3** 54 + 76 **4** 158 + 39 **5** 387 + 124

6 13 − 6 **7** 32 − 15 **8** 91 − 47 **9** 143 − 68 **10** 605 − 136

11 9 × 7 **12** 15 × 6 **13** 37 × 5 **14** 126 × 8 **15** 23 × 55

16 25 ÷ 5 **17** 91 ÷ 7 **18** 132 ÷ 3 **19** 243 ÷ 9 **20** 338 ÷ 13

Quick Test 2 – fractions and decimals

Use the chart to find equivalent fractions to each:

1 ½ = ¼ **2** ⅔ = % **3** ¾ = % **4** ⅔ = /₂₄ **5** ¾ = /₂₄

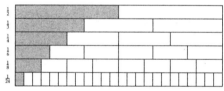

Which is biggest of each pair of fractions:

6 ⅔ or ⅓ **7** ⅔ or ½ **8** ⅝ or %₀ **9** ⅔ or ¾ **10** ⅝ or ⁷⁄₁₂

11 13.4 + 1.9 **12** 9.5 − 3.7 **13** 8.3 × 9 **14** 47.4 ÷ 3

Quick Test 3 – money

1 £15.49 + £7.63 **2** £31.50 − £7.75 **3** £9.54 × 8 **4** £38.15 ÷ 5

5 How much is 21 litres of petrol at 72.5 pence a litre?

6 How much change from £5 if I spend £3.62?

7 Driving lessons cost £27 each or four for £100. How much do I save?

8 If three pens and a pencil cost 54p and two of each costs 48p, how much is a pen and how much is a pencil?

Estimation and approximation

For many practical purposes, it can be useful not to work with numbers that are exact. For instance, when thinking about financial information for large organisations, it makes sense to give information in terms of whole millions of pounds, rather than down to the last pound and penny. If we re-write £16 185 251. 32 as £16m, we are **approximating**.

It can also help to simplify and speed up calculations to use rounded off figures. So to calculate £8205– £996 + £14179, we can do £8000 – £1000 + £14000, which is £21000. This is **estimating**.

?

Test Yourself

Quick Test 4 – estimating and approximating

1 8.9 × 11

2 £205.26 × 7

3 £9.63 shared between four people

4 15.7 ÷ 1.9

5 11.2 × 28.7

6 Production of series A cars increased from 76 741 to 183 207 and for series B cars from 91 423 to 255 981 in the same period. Which increased by the largest proportion?

Percentages

The next step in extending our repertoire comes by the addition (notice the mathematical metaphor!) of percentages.

Percentages are in fact, a special type of fraction. They are fractions expressed as hundredths.

So, for instance:

50% is the same as $\frac{50}{100}$
10% is the same as $\frac{10}{100}$

and so on.

We can also apply many of the same operations to percentages as to other fractions:

We can 'cancel them down'. This means we can simplify them by reducing the top and bottom (called the numerator and denominator, remember?) by the same factor.

So 50% is $\frac{50}{100}$

This can be simplified to $\frac{5}{10}$ (by dividing top and bottom by 10)

This can be further simplified to $\frac{1}{2}$ (by dividing top and bottom by 5)

So 50% is a half.

In a similar way, we can work out that:

10% is $\frac{1}{10}$
20% is $\frac{1}{5}$
25% is $\frac{1}{4}$
40% is $\frac{2}{5}$
60% is $\frac{3}{5}$
75% is $\frac{3}{4}$
80% is $\frac{4}{5}$

These simpler fractions can make it easier to perform percentage calculations in your head, very quickly.

? Test Yourself

Quick Test 5 – percentages

1% of £1 is 1p. What are:

1 1% of £2 **2** 1% of £5 **3** 1% of £12 **4** 1% of £217

5 2% of £30 **6** 10% of 60 miles **7** 25% of 48 hours **8** 60% of 60kg

9 A washing machine costs £540. How much would a 15% deposit be on this machine?

10 Reduce the price of a coffee maker of £42 by 20%

In this final test, we shall pose some numerical problems that involve some more sophisticated reasoning and problem solving skills.

Quick Test 6 – problem solving

1 Find a pair of numbers so that when I multiply them I get twice what I get when I add them.

2 If I give Karen a third of my bar of chocolate, she will have one more square than if I give her a quarter. How many squares in the chocolate?

3 Peter, Sue and Arnold all started with the same number of marbles. Peter lost half of his to Sue. Then Sue lost half of what she had to Arnold. Arnold finished up with 10 more marbles than Peter and Sue together. How many did they each start and finish with?

4 Calculate the shaded fraction of the third triangle.

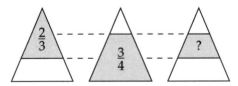

So, to sum up so far:

To be numerate, you need to be able to perform, and understand the four basic operations on whole numbers, and decimal numbers, to two decimal places (for money calculations). Additionally, it is useful to be able to divide up quantities into fractional parts, and to be able to calculate percentages.

Applications of basic numeracy

Statistics

As we have already said, in work, we need to process large amounts of data. Where this data is quantitative the branch of mathematics is called statistics. It involves the collection, organisation, and interpretation of quantitative data.

In a working environment, of course, data can be almost anything from:

- Number of units produced
- Sales
- Expenditure
- Costs
- Calls

And many, many more. It can also be data gained from research relating to people, products, markets, output and so on. In market and social research we can quantify opinions by applying scales:

Excellent	Good	Satisfactory	Poor
1	2	3	4

One of the first things we do with large quantities of data is to collect it into categories. This can be done with simple tally charts:

Vehicles observed passing a point on a motorway

HGV	vans	saloon cars	motorbikes
37	56	734	18

One of the most common ways of organising numerical data is into a frequency distribution. This involves splitting the whole distribution up into categories. The following example is the amounts spent by the first 60 people through a supermarket checkout:

£	Tally	Frequency
0–19	III	3
20–39	JHT JHT II	12
40–59	JHT JHT JHT JHT II	22
60–79	JHT JHT JHT II	16
80–99	JHT II	7

From this you can see that three people spent less than or equal to £19. Notice that all of the intervals are equal, and are £20 (0–19, 20–39, and so on).

One of the key statistics that can be calculated is called the average. Actually, there are three separate ways of calculating an average. For any set of figures, such as:

5   6   8   10   11

The mode is the most commonly appearing figure (where numbers appear more than once). The median is the figure in the middle, if they are all placed in ascending order. However, what most people call the average is technically known as the **mean.** It is the figure that represents if the total amount shared out equally.

We obtain this by adding all of the numbers together, and dividing by the number of numbers. In this case:

5 + 6 + 8 + 10 + 11 = 40

The mean is 40 divided by 5 which is 8.

In distributions like the one shown above, in our example, we can calculate the mean by assuming all of the figures in a band have the value of the mid point. Then we just multiply the frequency by the mid points, add them up, and divide by the number of values.

	Frequency (f)	Mid-point (x)	fx
0–19	3	9.5	28.5
20–39	12	29.5	354.0
40–59	22	49.5	1089.0
60–79	16	69.5	1112.0
80–99	7	89.5	626.5
	$\Sigma f = 60$		$\Sigma fx = 3210$

In symbols, the mean is:

$$\bar{x} = \frac{\Sigma fx}{\Sigma f} = \frac{3210}{60} = 53.5$$

(Σf means 'the sum of all the f's')

All frequency distributions can be illustrated as a diagram, so that we can get a visual idea of the distribution:

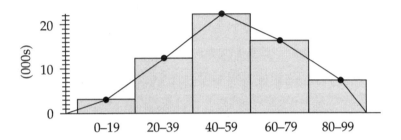

The extent to which distributions are 'spread out', can be described or calculated. In statistics, it is called the standard deviation. For most purposes it is never necessary to calculate this by hand, although it is useful to know that it exists and what it is.

A budget
In organisations a budget is a means of forecasting and controlling expenditure. Using a budget, an organisation, or a department can ensure that expenditure matches the needs of the business. It provides visibility and responsibility for the finance, and it can help to monitor activities on a regular basis. In principle, they are very simple.

Expenditure is divided into categories, and both the forecast (the budgeted amount), and the actual spending can be recorded next to each other for monitoring and comparison. The following is a very simple example:

	July	Aug	Sep	Oct
stationery	35	47	34	43
equipment	–	50	178	12
rents/rates	160	160	160	160
travel/subsistence	120	155	187	234
phone	–	196	–	–

This table could be made more sophisticated by adding the budgeted amount as well as the actual. This would enable differences (called variances) to be examined. It could also be made more useful (but more complicated) by adding last year, as a basis for comparison with this year.

This arrangement of figures in rows and columns is ideal for use and analysis with a **spreadsheet.** This is computer software which enables the processing of figures in the form of tables or grids. It can be used to carry out calculations, from the simple to the very complex:

- It can add up rows or columns to get totals
- It can perform calculations between numbers – for instance to work out percentages or averages
- It can help to make comparisons between figures

Moving averages
This is a special kind of average that is often used with figures that vary over a period of time. Take the following, for instance:

	1993				1994				1995		
Sales (£000's)	Q1	Q2	Q3	Q4	Q1	Q2	Q3	Q4	Q1	Q2	Q3	Q4
	27	47	58	39	33	56	82	46	47	74	94	62
Moving average		42.75	44.25	46.50	52.50	54.25	57.75	62.25	65.25	69.25		

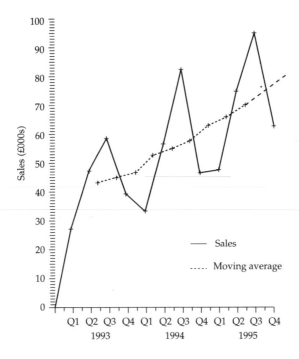

If you plot these on a graph you see that the figures rise and fall over the period. You may also see that there is some regularity to this – a seasonal increase in each quarter three period.

The moving average is able to show another kind of regularity, which is less easy to spot by eye. On the diagram, you can see that the moving average shows the general upward trend of the figures.

It is calculated by taking four figures (in this case Q1 + Q2 + Q3 + Q4 for 1993) and taking the average. The next average also takes four figures, but starts one further on (that is Q2 + Q3 + Q4 + Q1 of 1994). All subsequent averages are taken one quarter further on – which is why it is called 'moving'. To check your understanding, you could do the calculations for yourself, and compare them with the points on the trend line on the diagram.

Again, it is worth noticing that the actual arithmetic is very simple – just adding up and dividing by four. This kind of arithmetic and analysis could also be done very easily on a spreadsheet.

Pareto analysis
Pareto analysis is a simple statistical tool used in manufacturing and sales, to identify the 'vital few' from the 'trivial many'. The Pareto principle is often expressed as:

The 80:20 rule

For example, 80% of the sales come from 20% of the customers.

Pareto analysis begins with the collection of data. This table shows the source of common errors in an administration department.

Error	frequency
Wrong tel number	35
Typing	84
Filing	44
Lost document	6
Incomplete document	21
Not in diary	12
Others	4

To do the analysis, we re-order the table with the errors in rank order.

Error	total	cumulative	cumulative %
Typing	84	84	40.8
Filing	44	128	62.2
Wrong tel number	35	163	79.2
Incomplete document	21	184	89.4
Not in diary	12	196	95.2
Lost document	6	202	98.1
Others	4	206	100

The cumulative figure is the running total. So the 128 is made by 84 + 44, the 163 is made by 128 + 35, and so on. The cumulative percentage expresses this as a percentage of the total. So, $\frac{84}{206}$ (multiplied by 100, to make it a percentage) is 40.8%

The Pareto principle suggests that in such cases we get the biggest effect for the least effort by tackling the 20% of the factors that cause 80% of the problems. So just dealing with the first three categories of errors will eliminate 80% of them.

Summary

In this chapter, we have looked at the aspects of basic numeracy that are of most use in the working context.

We have looked at the basic operations of numeracy, and you have tried your hand at the Quick tests to assess your own attainment against each of these.

We have also looked at some of the most simple but most useful applications of basic numeracy. These include:

- Basic statistics
- Budgets
- Moving averages
- Pareto analysis

How numeracy is tested

As we have already described, for many people at work it is
bad enough that they lack skill or confidence in their
numerical abilities and knowledge. This is enough to
contend with. What compounds this situation for people in
this position (and for others), is that they may well have to
undergo some form of psychometric testing during their
career. Their fears are that they will not perform to their
best (often a self-fulfilling prophecy), or worse, that they
will be exposed as lacking the skills and knowledge that
they need. In this chapter we will look at all aspects of the
way that numeracy is assessed and tested at work. To do
this we will examine:

- Why numeracy is tested
- Psychometric testing
- Testing numeracy

Why numeracy is tested

The business case for testing aptitude and ability in
organisations is strong. Organisations are beginning to
realise that the talents of their staff (nowadays called
human capital) are one of, if not the primary resource they
have in a competitive environment. This has led to a focus
on competence. Organisations need to assess and evaluate
the competence of their staff before they can develop and
utilise it. Aptitude and ability are key aspects of the
capability of people. Hence the focus on psychometric
testing. Psychometric testing is increasingly being applied

in many of the human resource or human capital management functions. These include:

- Selection and recruitment
- Training needs analysis
- Training and development
- Team development
- Change and culture initiatives
- Performance management
- Career counselling

Such testing adds high quality information and objectivity to their analysis.

Within that general argument, we need to explain why the testing of numeracy is often a key part of that testing repertoire. There are two parts to the answer.

The first is that if we look at human capability from a psychometric point of view, aptitude and ability are the key to understanding our underlying and developed areas of skill. If you break down aptitude and ability into its constituent parts, numeracy, in its various forms is one of the key components. Numeracy then, along with verbal and abstract reasoning, is one of the basic building blocks of our aptitude and ability. This is why it is so often included in the testing process.

Related to that, the other part of the reason for including numeracy is the obvious practical aspect. As we have set out and described earlier in the book, numeracy is such an important part of the skill set required to perform many important functions in a real working environment. If people have to use these skills directly in their work, it is not surprising that they are part of the testing repertoire.

Psychometric testing

Having established the case for why psychometric tests are used to assess aptitide and ability, and numeracy as a part of that, we should explain a little more about what exactly psychometric tests are. One reason for this is that there is often some confusion about the name. This is because people often assume that all psychometric tests are about personality. They are not. Psychometric tests fall broadly into two categories. The first is those tests that examine our **typical** or habitual performance. These are our accumulated and learnt habits of behaviour. These are the tests of personality referred to above. If you would like to know more about these, you can find out by reading *'Test your Personality'* in this series.

The other type of tests are called tests of **maximum** performance. These are the tests of aptitude and ability. In general, they look at various aspects of our aptitude and ability.

Some tests look at our general, underlying fluid ability or intelligence, which was seen as an innate capability that underwrites our ability to learn and master most cognitive skills. IQ tests come into this category, although they are no longer widely used. Psychometricians (psychologists interested in measuring ability) use the notion of 'fluid intelligence' to explain that our ability to learn or master one specific area is related to our ability to master any other.

There are tests that focus on and attempt to measure this

fluid intelligence. The line of reasoning is clear. If we know your score on such a test, we can infer your ability to perform a whole range of cognitive tasks. That is then a good basis for predicting other abilities.

Aptitude

There is another school of thought that says that we should look at more specific aspects of general cognitive ability. As well as giving more detailed information, these specific abilities are more closely work related, and from them we can predict more accurately a person's likely performance in work tasks.

These measure natural ability or potential particularly to learn a skill or a set of skills. They focus on our underlying ability, but applied in specific areas. They should not require specialist knowledge or learning.

So what does get measured? Here are some typical things that get measured.

Abstract reasoning – assesses the ability to understand the relationships between shapes and figures

Verbal reasoning – assesses understanding of words and relationships between words

Numerical reasoning – assesses the ability to operate on numbers and numerical concepts

Critical reasoning – assesses the ability to draw inferences from data of various kinds

Accuracy tests – assess the ability to check or classify information Checking computer statements or syntax would be an example.

Other, more specific types of test include :

Mechanical reasoning

Spatial reasoning

Hand eye coordination

Attainment
The aptitude tests are distinct from attainment tests. These measure skills and/or knowledge which have already been learned or acquired. They test the ability to put that knowledge to use. This is intelligence applied and learnt in a specific context. They can test quite specific tasks and abilities and can be highly work related.

Examples might include:

- Typing tests
- The new written test for learner drivers
- Spelling tests
- Grammar and punctuation tests

In numeracy, such tests would measure our ability to perform certain specified operations or processes. The Quick Tests in the previous chapter are a good guide to your performance in the attainment of the most important aspects of numeracy.

We should also mention that some of the tests that are apparently tests of aptitude, can also involve a substantial learnt element. This means that strictly speaking, they are also tests of attainment. Tests of mechanical ability fall into this category where aptitude and attainment overlap.

The three categories:

- Verbal
- Numerical
- Abstract

are the ones focused on in most organisations. They also together comprise a rounded and comprehensive selection of a person's general ability as it relates to work based skills.

This is not to say that in some specific jobs, other abilities may not be required. However, this trio seem to be the ones that are required, to a greater or lesser degree in most jobs.

Testing for aptitude and ability
Aptitude and ability are tested differently from some of the topics in the other books in the series. This is because they are invariably tested by psychometric test. Here we explain what we mean by a psychometric test, and how aptitude and ability are different, even from other kinds of psychometric tests.

What are psychometric tests? The British Psychological Society describes a psychometric test as:

'an instrument designed to produce a quantitative assessment of some psychological attribute or attributes.'

For the most part 'an instrument' means a paper and pencil test involving a series of multiple choice questions.

One of the keys to the success and wide usage of psychometric tests is that they are objective. This objectivity comes about because the tests have certain characteristics in common. Good tests should have the following characteristics:

They are **standardised.** This means that your score should be compared to those of a 'normal' group. Any score you get should tell you how you performed in relation to the average for the compared group. This is often expressed in special measures (like percentiles or sten scores). However, what you need to know most is how you compare with the average for the group as a whole.

Reliable. They should give scores in a consistent way so that your score is independent of factors like when and where you take the test. The conditions in which the tests are administered is standardised. This includes the instructions that are given to the candidates

Valid. They should measure a psychological coherent attribute – ie they should measure what they say they measure. With tests of aptitude and ability this means either they should tell you something valid about a general ability, or the specific ability relates closely to real performance in the job (this is called the predictive value).

Fair. They should give equal opportunity to all people to score accurately against the attribute tested.

In addition, aptitude and ability tests involve the following:

- They are objective – they are not based on opinion or judgement but facts
- There are right and wrong answers (unlike personality tests)
- They are paper and pencil tests – usually multiple-choice
- They are often timed, to ensure accurate comparison between test takers.

Testing numeracy

In this section, we look at the various aspects of numeracy that are frequently tested, describe them, and set out some examples to show you what to expect.

Tests of numerical reasoning look at the ability to work with numbers. The attainment aspect tests those things that you have learnt to do over a lifetime of schooling and education.

However, the aptitude tests are looking at your ability to work with numerical concepts and should not be too influenced by how much you did or did not learn at school/college/university. It is not necessarily the same as the ability to be good at mathematics, which requires a whole range of other skills as well as substantial knowledge of particular mathematical concepts. This is good news for those people who feel that they did not do themselves justice in maths at school.

On the whole, you should be able to score well in aptitude tests without having reached a high level of attainment in formal education in maths.

Attainment
Some jobs require particular routines or arithmetic processes, and many of these can be learnt. That means that they can also be tested for. Examples would include:

- Ability to perform basic calculations or operations
- Knowledge of basic arithmetic processes such as estimating quantities, or calculating percentages

Aptitude testing

This relies less on particular arithmetical operations and more on the ability to spot relationships and work with numbers.

The questions in such tests can take a number of forms. Typical questions include:

Series – these involve working out the 'rule' by which subsequent numbers are derived, and calculating the next one.

Example:

4 7 10 13 —

The numbers are obtained by adding three to the previous number (or term), so the next one is $13 + 3$ or 16

Example:

2 3 5 9 —

Each term is obtained by doubling and taking 1 away, so the next term is $2 \times 9 - 1$, which is 17.

Relationships – these involve spotting the relationship between two numbers, and applying it to the next pair.

Example:

3 is to 12 as 8 is to

16 24 20 64 32 36

To get 12 from 3 you multiply by 4, so 8 times 4 is 32. (source: Psytech International)

Basic calculations – simple application of arithmetic operations to solve simple problems.

Example:

If £1 buys 9 francs how much will you get for £20?

90 160 180 1800 900 209

The answer is 20 times 9 francs, which is 180 francs.

Numerical critical reasoning – this involves drawing conclusions from numerical information. It uses a higher and more sophisticated set of skills than the previous examples, because questions require understanding, analysing, comparing and interpreting data. In tests of numerical critical reasoning this is usually presented in the form of a table.

Example:

EXAMPLE TABLE (WOMEN)				
% of Women, within each Age Group, citing each Characteristic as the most important feature of a car.				
CHARACTERISTIC	20–29	30–39	40–49	50–59	60–69
Performance	18	12	8	10	5
Economy	17	24	29	28	32
Reliability	34	32	24	27	35
Safety	18	30	32	31	27
Design	13	2	7	4	1
(Source: CRTB, Psytech)					

For women, which is the least important feature of a car?

Performance economy reliability safety design cannot say

To get the answer to this you need to assess how important each characteristic is for all women (because age is not mentioned in the question). To do this you have to add the percentages in each age group across the rows. The smallest one is the least important feature, and in this case this is design. However, many people won't add the figures up, because they can see at a glance that the numbers for design are much lower than the other characteristics, for all age groups. To test your understanding of this idea, can you work out which is the most important feature?

These examples should give you an idea of what you should expect in tests, and the types of items you might see in real tests. Before going on to have a try at testing yourself, there are a few other things you should think about if you are going to undergo testing yourself.

How scores are interpreted

Before we turn to your own test, we should explain how scores are used and interpreted when real, commercial tests are used. Most people, when they take any kind of test, are interested to know what their 'score' is. There are underlying assumptions here that are common to most people. These are:

- The result will be a single number or score
- That the score is just the number of right answers, perhaps expressed as a percentage

In fact, both these assumptions tend to be wrong. Of course, as we have pointed out previously, aptitude and ability tests are based on right and wrong answers, but it is not the number of right answers that is the most important thing. As we have also described, what is important about these tests is that the scores are standardised. What this means is that your scores are compared to those of a known group of people. Distributions of scores for a known group of people are called norms. The known group of people itself might be the general population; graduates; managers; people in a particular organisation.

The standardisation works in the following way. When you have a group of people taking a test, the scores will be distributed from low to high. Invariably, these scores, when graphed will look like this:

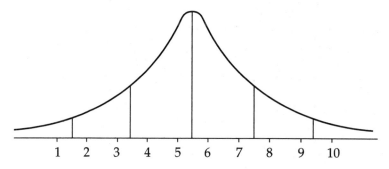

This is called the normal (or 'bell' curve) and is very common for many naturally occuring measures. What happens then is that this distribution is 'carved up' into segments. These segments can be based on numbers. So, if the distribution is carved into hundredths, they are called percentiles. If it is carved into ten, they are called sten (or standard tens) scores. Your score, then, is not given as a raw score (such as 25 out of 40, for instance). Your score is compared to the distribution. If percentiles are used, the 80th percentile does not mean you scored 80%, but that you scored more than 80% of the norm population. In other words, the feedback is comparing your performance to that of the rest of the normed group.

In many cases, this is not even done by numbers, but by banding, or slicing the distribution into categories (as shown in the diagram above). So quite often the feedback you get will not be in the form of a number but might be in the form of a statement like:

'in the top band'

'average'

'as well as most people ...'

and other such similar statements.

If you think about your own education history, and you evaluated your own numerical aptitude and ability, if you could be reasonably sure you are 'above average', 'average', or 'below average', this is all the information you need.

In terms of the test we present in this book, the scores have not been standardised. We have suggested that the scores are placed in bands (low, medium and high) which will give you a fair indication, but not an exact comparison to a known group. For that, you would have to complete a commercial test.

Summary

We have summarised here the information that is emphasised throughout the book. The key message is that because numeracy is such an important foundation to many of the skills and processes that we use in work, it is not surprising that organisations need to know more about the skills and competence of their current and prospective employees. Psychometric testing is one way to do this.

We have described how aptitude and ability are tested, including the main aspects such as verbal, abstract as well as numerical aptitude. We have set out what psychometric tests are and what they do.

To help you to 'get a feel' for real tests, we have described and illustrated with examples exactly what the questions (items) look like in tests of attainment, aptitude and numerical reasoning.

Finally, we have shown how tests are scored and how those scores are interpreted.

The numeracy test

Preparing for testing

One important way in which you can develop yourself in relation to aptitude and ability testing is to make sure that you perform to the best of your ability in a real testing situation. For many people, ignorance of the process and anxiety during the testing mean that they do not perform to their full potential.

The testing process
The first thing you should be aware of is what to expect in the testing process itself. Here are a few simple guidelines as to the steps involved:

1. Familiarise yourself with the tests themselves.
    As we have already mentioned, it is quite normal for test publishers to provide practice and familiarisation material. Don't be afraid to ask for this if it is not provided automatically. Failing that, you are entitled to ask about the nature of the test – what kinds of test; what it/they comprise; if there are any descriptions or guidelines, and so on.
2. Find out about the arrangements.
    This should include the obvious and basic considerations such as the start time and the location. You should also be forewarned of the duration of the test(s) themselves. Check if there are any special considerations, or if you need to bring any equipment. (You shouldn't need to, but checking is always a reassurance).
3. The testing.
    The testing itself should be done in an environment that is

conducive. That is, it should be comfortable, and it should be free from disturbance. To aid standardisation, all candidates should do the testing in the same conditions, preferebly at the same time. There should be a trained and qualified test administrator. He/she should:

- Provide the appropriate materials
- Describe the context, purpose and process
- Read the instructions
- Invigilate the test (including timing it if appropriate)
- Arrange for the scoring to be done

4. Feedback.

You should always be made aware of if, how and when feedback will be given. There are circumstances where feedback is not given. This is sometimes the case, for instance, in the testing of external candidates for recruitment. However, in many cases feedback will only be given if it is requested, and so it is always worthwhile making the request. Where feedback is given, it should be constructive and confidential. The opportunity to discuss the results should always be offered.

Preparing for testing

Because testing does involve anxiety for many, you can use your preparation time as an opportunity to present yourself for the test in the best frame of mind possible. These are some ideas that might assist you in achieving that:

1. Get clued up.

Use the opportunity to find out as much as you can about the purpose; the nature of the tests; the timings, and so on. As mentioned above, use the opportunity to ask for practice material if it is available. This way there should be no surprises on the day.

2. Familiarisation.

   Use what practice material is available (or the nearest you can find). This has two benefits. The first is to help your brain get used to thinking in the right kind of ways required for the test. The second is really about reassurance. Again, once you know what to expect, and you have 'had a go', it means that there are no unpleasant surprises, and this helps you to get the best out of yourself.

3. Manage your state of mind.

   This involves a number of elements. Certainly you should arrive at the day in the right state of mind. Make sure you have had a few good nights sleep before the day. Relaxing activity the day/night before always helps. This is achieved in different ways by different people, but can involve exercise, leisure or other means of relaxation. Finally, use every opportunity to give yourself positive messages. There is no doubt that if you tell yourself that you will make a mess of it, you are more than half way to doing just that! Many people have supportive friends or loved ones who can help in this.

4. The day itself.

   Time your arrival just right. Being late and flustered will not help, but neither will being there an hour before with nothing positive to do. The key is to be physically relaxed, whilst being mentally alert.

5. The test itself.

   It is difficult to give very general advice because tests differ so much. In approach to the test, it is better to do the questions in order. You should do those that are easy to do, or at least not too difficult. In a short timed test, it is usually a mistake to spend a long time poring over a question that you may get wrong anyway. The best rule is to do as much as you can do well straight away, then use any time left to do what else you can.

Testing your numeracy

As we have explained in previous chapters, we have made a distinction between attainment, which is related to how well you have learnt the basic operations of numeracy, and numerical aptitude. You had the opportunity in chapter two to look at and to assess your own level of attainment. Here we test your aptitude in the same way that it would be done in many of the psychometric tests that you could undergo.

Even so, we will look at two aspects of that aptitude. In the first, we look at your general **aptitude** in relation to numeracy. This is the ease and accuracy with which you can process and manipulate numbers. In the second, we look at your **numerical reasoning**. This is more to do with the way you can analyse, interpret and draw conclusions from tables of numerical information.

The tests use the kinds of items (questions) that are used in such tests, and the format is also very much the same. Although these tests are not timed, (as real ones would be), bear in mind that time is a factor, and you should do them as quickly as you can.

? Test Yourself

Numerical aptitude

(answers on page 76)

Sequences

What is the next number in each of these sequences?

1 1 2 4 8 ?

2 1 4 7 10 ?

3 11 9 7 5 ?

4 1 4 9 16 25 ?

5 3 7 15 31 ?

For the next set, one of the numbers in the sequence is missing. Choose from the available options, which one you think is the correct number.

6 17 15 ? 11   12 10 13

7 2.5 5.0 ? 10   8 7.5 10 7

8 2 3 5 ? 17   7 11 9 13

9 4 5 9 ? 14   10 13 11

10 8.4 8.1 7.8 ? 7.2   7.4 7.5 7.6

Relationships

1 7 is to 1 as 11 is to
       7 5 3 6

2 which is the odd one out?
       6 12 15 16

3 3 is to 9 as 5 is to
       12 25 45

4 ¾ is to .75 as ⅖ is to
       .4 .5 .6 .35

5 2.48 is to 1.24 as 6.24 is to
  3.48 3.12 3.24

6 2 is to ½ as 3 is to
  0.3 1.5 ⅓ ⅔

7 what comes next?
  555544433
  3 1 2

8 .6 is to 3 as .8 is to
  .6 4 3 5

9 27 is to 3 as 81 is to
  7 3 9 13

10 25% is to ¼ as 60% is to
  ½ ¼ ⅗ ⅙

Numerical critical reasoning

The table shows the percentages of questions answered
correctly by people in various countries, when asked to do a
simple maths test.

Question	UK	France	Holland	Japan
1	70	81	85	94
2	83	94	93	97
3	56	76	85	80
4	80	86	95	96
5	54	73	85	83
6	65	88	84	88
7	54	61	81	86

1 Who scored lowest on question 4?

2 'UK scored the lowest on every question'. True or false?

3 'Nobody scored as high as Japan on any question'. True or false?

4 Which was the hardest question?

5 'Britain's highest score was lower than Holland's lowest score.' True or false?

In a survey, people responded as shown to the question:

'Television is better now than 10 years ago.'

Response	All	Men	Women	18–24s	55+
Agree	23	24	22	27	21
Disagree	72	73	71	69	74
No opinion	5	3	6	5	4

6 'Most people think that TV is worse (or no better) now than ten years ago.' True or false?

7 Are young people more or less likely to disagree with the statement than old people?

8 'More men agree with the statement than women.' True or false?

9 Were men more or less likely to disagree with the statement than young people?

10 Are you more likely to agree with the statement if you are a woman or if you are young?

These tables show the percentage of men and women in each age group who rated each characteristic as the most important feature of a new house:

MEN Characteristic	20–35	36–50	51+
Price	55	42	35
Location	20	25	30
Condition	25	33	35

WOMEN Characteristic	20–35	36–50	51+
Price	50	35	28
Location	25	35	40
Condition	25	30	22

11 For older women, which is the most important feature?

12 Which characteristic becomes increasingly less important with age?

13 For the youngest age group, do more men or women rate location as the most important characteristic?

14 Which characteristic increases with age for both men and women?

15 'Twice as many young women rate price as important as middle aged men (36–50) rate location.' True or false?

Interpreting your test scores

Having now completed the tests, the first thing to do is to score them up, using the answers at the back of the book. We shall treat the scores for attainment – the Quick Test scores, differently to the aptitude scores in this chapter.

Before we get to the scores themselves, you should be prepared to consider your scores in their true perspective. We have tried to make the tests as accurate and as realistic as possible, but in a number of ways, they are no substitute for knowledge of our real experience of the world.

You can make some assessment of your skills from other factors, as well as the tests themselves.

1   **Educational experience and attainment.** What was the highest level of schooling or education that you have achievement in a numerate subject? If, for instance, you have done a statistics course at college or university, regardless of your aptitude level, you may, by dint of application and hard work, have achieved quite a high level of knowledge and competence in some important skills.

2   **Work experience.** Using a similar line of reasoning, necessity and hard work could have helped you to learn important skills and processes (such as budgeting, or interpreting sales figures) during your working life.

3   **Life experience.** Many people, including those who convince themselves that they are poor at mathematics, are able to learn sophisticated skills to enable them to manage their normal lives. Running bank accounts, tax self-assessment, holding investments, buying and monitoring mortgages, budgeting and planning for holidays, running a household account, are all things that need a high level of numerical skill.

You should take account of your whole range of skills to balance your interpretation of the test scores. Only in this way can you get a complete picture to balance against your score.

But of course, there is also a great deal of value in doing the tests, and in the scores themselves, (otherwise you would not have bought the book)! These advantages include:

1   You will 'know where you stand' against important measures and benchmarks
2   You will be better prepared for any psychometric testing that you might have to undergo.
3   You will have had some excellent practice and will have helped to develop your skills and fluency
4   You should know where you are good (as well as where you are less good), and this should help with your confidence

All of these factors should be borne in mind when you look at your scores.

Attainment

With these, it is the raw scores that are important. They should speak for themselves. They should help you to identify which skills and knowledge you do have, as opposed to those where you do less well.

For the latter, if you wish to improve, there are really only two things to take account of. The first is finding out how the processes should be done properly, and this involves checking up in books or other sources. The second is just about practising until you are accurate and confident.

Aptitude

As we explained in the previous chapter, scores on these tests are not usually given or interpreted in terms of how many you got right or wrong. They are interpreted in terms of how well you score compared to other groups of people.

Our particular tests have not been standardised – you would have to do a commercially available test for that information.

However, you can get a good idea by banding your score in the following way:

Add together the two aptitude scores to get a single score out of 20. Your score is:

0–8 Low. This suggest you are lacking confidence and fluency in manipulating numbers. You may find it difficult to process and use numbers in some contexts. You may find it difficult or are very slow to pick and learn new processes with numbers.

9–13 Medium. You have a good base level of skill and aptitude. You are likely to do as well as most people in picking up skills and using numbers in most working contexts.

14–20 High. You show real fluency and a higher than average aptitude. This is likely to mean that you find it fairly easy to develop skills working with numerical ideas and quantitative information.

Numerical critical reasoning
Here there is a single score out of 15. You can band them as follows:

0–6 Low. You may find it quite difficult to organise, analyse and interpret complex numerical data. Drawing conclusions from graphs and tables of figures may not be your strength.

7–11 Medium. You should be as good as most people at processing and interpreting numerical data.

11–15 High. You are likely to find it easy to process and draw conclusions from even complex numerical and quantitative information.

Summary

You should now have a good idea of where you stand, in relation to attainment, and in terms of aptitude. Take time to think about your scores, and balance this with other information about your approach and experience with numeracy, as suggested here.

For those who wish to develop and practice their basic numeracy skills, the following chapter should help.

Developing your numerical skills

In this section, we shall complement and consolidate on the work of the previous chapters by giving you the opportunity to develop and practise your skills related to basic numeracy. To do this we shall look at:

- Basic mental arithmetic
- Practice in essential skills

Basic mental arithmetic

We start with the most basic skills, but with the most sophisticated equipment for the job – your own brain! If you have spent time in your life hiding from numbers, and avoiding quantitative information – now is the time to start fighting back. You'll find it easier than you ever thought.

By laying down a strong foundation of the most simple but basic processes and concepts you will be able to cope better with the more advanced requirements for handling numeracy in the working environment.

The primary purpose of this chapter is to help you to get friendly with numbers, and to be able to perform some basic but important operations fluently and confidently in your head. But why bother with mental arithmetic?

There are three basic reasons:

1 For many people, it is precisely this ability to operate fluently with numbers that was missing from their education first time around.
2 It is fast and efficient as it helps you to develop and use

the incredible computing power of the brain. Developing
and practising such strategies prevents you having to
resort to, or invent torturous longhand algorithms, or
having to remember complicated rules quite so often.
3   By developing skills we also develop confidence.

A final reason for developing your mental processing
capacity is that:

It is easy and it is learnable

Get friendly with the times tables
This is a great place to start. Some people, for various
reasons, somehow forgot to learn their multiplication tables
with the confidence and speed of recall that they now need
or would like. Of course, it's never too late, and there is
little substitute for practice.

However, one way to get friendly with them and
understand them a bit more is to look at the patterns that
occur in these tables. There are many patterns there to be
discovered, and they all help to remember them more easily.

One way to see such patterns is to put the numbers 1–100
in a 10 × 10 grid.

1	2	3	4	5	6	7	8	9	10
11	12	13	14	15	16	17	18	19	20
21	22	23	24	25	26	27	28	29	30
31	32	33	34	35	36	37	38	39	40
41	42	43	44	45	46	47	48	49	50
51	52	53	54	55	56	57	58	59	60
61	62	63	64	65	66	67	68	69	70
71	72	73	74	75	76	77	78	79	80
81	82	83	84	85	86	87	88	89	90
91	92	93	94	95	96	97	98	99	100

If you imagine shading in the multiples of 2 – the numbers in the 2 times table, the pattern is simple and obvious but striking.

What does the pattern for the 5 times table look like? Can you visualise it? If not, use this blank grid to check it out.

1	2	3	4	5	6	7	8	9	10
11	12	13	14	15	16	17	18	19	20
21	22	23	24	25	26	27	28	29	30
31	32	33	34	35	36	37	38	39	40
41	42	43	44	45	46	47	48	49	50
51	52	53	54	55	56	57	58	59	60
61	62	63	64	65	66	67	68	69	70
71	72	73	74	75	76	77	78	79	80
81	82	83	84	85	86	87	88	89	90
91	92	93	94	95	96	97	98	99	100

How about the 9 times table? The 3 times table is similar.

The 6 times table is interesting. Can you see the 'knights move' in it?

There are other ways to see patterns in tables. Take the 9 times table:

$1 \times 9 = 9$
$2 \times 9 = 18$
$3 \times 9 = 27$
$4 \times 9 = 36$
$5 \times 9 = 45$
$6 \times 9 = 54$
$7 \times 9 = 63$
$8 \times 9 = 72$
$9 \times 9 = 81$

Notice that the leading digit 'counts up' (0, 1, 2, etc)

The trailing digit counts down (9, 8, etc)

Notice that when you add the digits, they add up to 9:

$1 + 8 = 9$

$2 + 7 = 9$

and so on.

It looks like this pattern will stop at:

$12 \times 9 = 108$

But $1 + 0 + 8 = 9$

The pattern carries on ...

Does this appreciation of the pattern help you to remember the 9 times table more easily? If you think that it does, then you can look at patterns in other tables. For instance, look at the last digits in the numbers in the 4 times table (4, 8, 12, and so on). There are many patterns to explore, all of which help you to get to know the tables more easily.

A familiarity with the basic multiplying relationships of numbers up to 9×9 is the foundation on which all arithmetic is based. The better you know them the easier all the rest is. Having started to get that you can now start to put it to use.

Halving and quartering
We can start with a simple, but useful skill that begins to get you used to processing numbers and developing the 'unconscious competence' that is the basis for real confidence.

Start the habit of halving and quartering numbers mentally when you come across them and you will soon devise your own strategies for doing it with speed and accuracy.

To halve 140

We can either do:

Half of 100 = 50

Half of 40 = $\underline{20}$ +
$\underline{70}$

or we can reason:

$2 \times 7 = 14$

so $2 \times 70 = 140$

Quartering is just half, then half again.

Now try halving these:

120 260 370 1800 92 58 132 156 2420

Try quartering:

36 44 60 104 152

Try some bigger ones:

976 2240 1240 28320

Subtraction
This is one of the most basic operations, and it can be done much more efficiently and fluently using mental processes than with written algorithms.

You can see dramatic evidence for this if you watch a darts match in any pub! But how do these players manage such sophisticated calculations so easily and quickly? The answer is threefold:

1. They know the relationships between numbers by constant familiarity
2. By developing personalised methods that work
3. Practice, practice, practice ...

One of the simplest methods for doing subtraction is called **the shopkeeper method**.

To do 48 − 25 we can count:

25 to 30 is 5 +
30 to 40 is 10 +
40 to 48 is 8
Answer   23

Use this method to calculate:

30 − 18, 52 − 16, 45 − 13, 63 − 29

Try some more difficult ones:

132 − 55, 111 − 49, 35 − 67, 289 − 37

The 'Nines' method
We often need to subtract from 100 or 1000. However, the written method makes this difficult (do you remember 'borrowing one and paying back'?)

Instead of doing 100 − 37 by the 'old' school method, we can do:

99 −
37
62

and add the one back to make 62 + 1 which is 63.

The only difference with subtracting from 1000 is that you use 999 and then add the one back.

Try taking these from 100:

25 17 49 63

Try taking these from 1000:

333 64 128 354

Multiplication
This is the most used operation in all of arithmetic. As a requisite you need to have developed confidence with the tables up to 9×9 (see the first section for ideas). For the more mature among you who remember having to do the 11 and 12 times table, it was a throwback to our old currency system, and is not now necessary.

Again, there is an equivalent to the shopkeeper method. To calculate 8×13, we do:

$8 \times 10 =$ 80+
$8 \times 3 =$ $\underline{24}$
    $\underline{104}$

For numbers just short of a round 10, there is a sort of 'reverse' shopkeeper method. To do 3×19, we do:

$3 \times 20 =$ 60

less $3 \times 1 =$ $\underline{3}$ (the difference between 20 and 19)
    $\underline{57}$

To do 7×28, we do:

7×30 $\quad = 210$ (notice $7 \times 3 = 21$ so $7 \times 30 = 210$)
less $7 \times 2 = \underline{14}$ $\quad$ (2 is the difference between 28 and 30)
$\qquad\qquad\quad \overline{196}$

Now try these:

8×9 $\quad 5 \times 19$ $\quad 7 \times 17$ $\quad 12 \times 28$ $\quad 11 \times 57$

Using large numbers
The calculation 7×30 above gives us a clue that large numbers can be dealt with easily if they can be treated like small numbers. This is important because many people are 'blind' to large numbers and find it difficult (at first) to cope with scale. The way to deal with this is to treat them as multiples of a larger unit. Remember, the leftmost number is always the most significant.

Try to get used to saying (and thinking)

45 000 is just 45 (thousand)

Large numbers can often be approximated, for some purposes:

1 252 199

is (about) 1.25 million

It may help sometimes to change units:

£0.5 million = £ 500 000 or £ 500K

Now try these by writing them out in full:

£ 0.4m £0.95m £ 0.12m £0.01m £2.1m £0.35m

Try to find some and change them the other way round for practice.

Percentages
Percentages are a great way of practising. They are also important as they account for a great number of applications.

Start by calculating 10% of amounts.

You do this by moving the decimal point, because 10% is equivalent to one tenth – the same as dividing by 10.

10% of £4 is 40p

10% of £2.60 is 26p

10% of £90.50 is £9.05

Now try these, by finding 10% of:

£6 £18 £4.80 £ 260 £ 362 £ 54. 90 £500K

You can calculate 1% by doing one tenth (10%) and one tenth again (1%), or by directly dividing by 100.

Find 1% of the original amounts in the previous exercise:

Many common and useful percentages can be calculated using simple mental methods. For example:

To get 50% you just halve the amount

To get 25% you halve and halve again

To get 20% you do 10% and double it.

To get 15% you do 10%, halve it and add (it takes less time to do than to say!)

For example, to find 15% of £36:

10% is   £3.60 +
5% is   £1.80
15% is   £5.40

Find 50%, 25%, 20% and 15% of these:

£18 £240 £6.20 £60 000 £1.2m

Now check whether your speed is improving. Try devising some methods of your own for doing these:

25% 20% 11% 2% 7½%

and use them on these:

£5 £42 £2.40 £79 £ 120 £5620

Now you should be able to use these skills to begin to make comparative judgements about amounts, like the following:

Is 10% of £180 bigger than 25% of £70?

Practice in the essential skills

It is only by continuously using our skills that we develop speed, accuracy and confidence with them. Here are a few strategies that may help you to continue to develop basic numeracy skills:

1 *Mental arithmetic.* Use the ideas from this section to 'doodle' with numbers as you come across them. Use a calculator to check your accuracy.

2 *In work.* Take an interest in the more numerical aspects of your work. Take figures and tables away, and 'do your homework' in the privacy of your own home, and

in your own time, until you understand what is going on.

3 *At home.* Take an interest in, and follow up with the numeracy aspects of your own life – bank accounts, home budgets, mortgages, and so on. Try doing some of the calculations for yourself. Use resources like your daily newspaper, where there is a huge amount of information presented in numerical form.

3 *'Phone a friend'* Find people you know and trust to help and explain things you do not understand.

4 *Follow up.* There are many sources of help and further learning. There are many books available to follow up on specialised topics. There are also organisations like The Adults Basic Skills Agency, who can help with advice, resources and assessment.

Summary

In this chapter, we have given you some direct ideas and help in developing your own skills, and some ideas on how to follow up and further develop those skills. You might like now to go back to the earlier chapters to refresh your knowledge, or to have another go at some of the tests.

We have constantly emphasised that improvement is not a single hit process, and you need to practise and continually engage with the numerical information you come across at work or elsewhere.

Answers

Quick Test 1 – four rules
1 24   **2** 43   **3** 130   **4** 197   **5** 511   **6** 7   **7** 17   **8** 44   **9** 75
10 469   **11** 63   **12** 90   **13** 185   **14** 1008   **15** 1265   **16** 5
17 13   **18** 44   **19** 27   **20** 26

Quick Test 2 – fractions and decimals
1 $\frac{3}{4}$ **2** $\frac{4}{5}$ **3** $\frac{5}{8}$ **4** $\frac{16}{24}$ **5** $\frac{18}{24}$ **6** $\frac{2}{3}$ **7** $\frac{3}{5}$ **8** $\frac{9}{10}$ **9** $\frac{3}{4}$ **10** $\frac{5}{8}$
11 15.3   **12** 5.8   **13** 74.7   **14** 15.8

Quick Test 3 – money
1 £23.12   **2** £23.75   **3** £76.32   **4** 7.63   **5** £15.22½   **6** £1.38
7 £8 **8** pen – 15p, pencil – 9p.

Quick Test 4 – estimation
1 $9 \times 11 = 99$ **2** $7 \times £200 = 1400$ **3** $10 - 4 = 2.50$
4 $16 - 2 = 8$ **5** $11 \times 30 = 330$ **6** 80 000 to 180 000 is two
and a bit times. 90 000 to 250 000 (or 260 000) is nearly three
times.

Quick Test 5 – percentages
1 2p   **2** 5p   **3** 12p   **4** 2.17   **5** 60p   **6** 6miles   **7** 12 hours
8 36 kg   **9** £81   **10** £33.60

Quick Test 6 – problems
1 3 and 6, but there are many examples   **2** 12 squares

3	Peter	Sue	Arnold
start	20	20	20
finish	10	15	35

4 $\frac{5}{12}$

Numerical aptitude

Sequences
1 16   **2** 13   **3** 3   **4** 36   **5** 63   **6** 13   **7** 7.5   **8** 9   **9** 10   **10** 7.5

Relationships
1 5   **2** 16   **3** 25   **4** .6   **5** 3.12   **6** ⅓   **7** 2   **8** 4   **9** 9   **10** ⅗

Numerical critical reasoning
1 UK   **2** true   **3** not true (France scored as high on Q6)
4 3   **5** false   **6** true   **7** less   **8** true   **9** more   **10** young
11 location   **12** price   **13** women   **14** location   **15** true

Useful addresses

The British Psychological Society (BPS), 48 Princess Road
East, Leicester LE1 7DR. Telephone: 0116 254 9568, Fax:
0116 247 0787.

The Institute of Management (IM), Management House,
Cottingham Road, Corby, Northants, NN17 1TT. Telephone:
01536 204222

The Institute of Personnel and Development (IPD), IPD
House, Camp Rd, London, SW19 4UX. Telephone: 0208 971
9000

Basic Skills Agency, 7th Floor, Commonwealth House, 1–19
New Oxford Street, London, WC1A 1NV. Telephone: 0207
405 4017 www.basic-skills.co.uk

Test suppliers and publishers

Oxford Psychologists Press Ltd, Lambourne House,
311–321 Banbury Road, Oxford, OX2 7JH. Telephone: 01865
311353

The Psychological Corporation, Foots Cray, High Street,
Sidcup, DA14 5HP

Psytech International Ltd, The Grange, Church Road,
Pulloxhill, Beds, MK45 5HE. Telephone: 01525 720003

Saville & Holdsworth Ltd, 3 AC Court, High Street, Thames
Ditton, Surrey, KT7 0SR. Telephone: 0208 398 4170

The Test Agency, Cray House, Woodlands Road, Henley on Thames, Oxon, RG9 4AE. Telephone: 01491 413413

Further reading

Mason, Roger (1993) *Finance for Non-Financial Managers in a Week*. Hodder & Stoughton Educational.

Secrett, Malcolm (1993) *Successful Budgeting in a Week*. Hodder & Stoughton Educational.

Rowntree, Derek (1991) *Statistics without Tears: a primer for non-mathematicians*. Penguin Books.

Further *Test Your ...* titles from Hodder & Stoughton and the Institute of Management, all at £6.99

0 340 78006 1	Test Your Personality	❏
0 340 78050 9	Test Your Management Style	❏
0 340 78169 9	Test Your Management Skills	❏
0 340 78208 0	Test Your Leadership Skills	❏
0 340 78287 0	Test Your Financial Awareness	❏
0 340 78288 9	Test Your Literacy	❏
0 340 78290 0	Test Your Potential	❏

All Hodder & Stoughton books are available from your local bookshop or can be ordered direct from the publisher. Just tick the titles you want and fill in the form below. Prices and availability subject to change without notice.

To: Hodder & Stoughton Ltd, Cash Sales Department, Bookpoint, 78 Milton Park, Abingdon, Oxon OX14 4TD. If you have a credit card you may order by
telephone – 01235 400414
      fax – 01235 400454
E-mail address: orders@bookpoint.co.uk

Please enclose a cheque or postal order made payable to Bookpoint Ltd to the value of the cover price and allow the following for postage and packaging:

UK & BFPO: £4.30 for one book; £6.30 for two books; £8.30 for three books.

OVERSEAS & EIRE: £4.80 for one book; £7.10 for 2 or 3 books (surface mail).

Name: ....

Address: ....

....

....

If you would prefer to pay by credit card, please complete:

Please debit my Visa/Mastercard/Diner's Card/American Express (delete as appropriate) card no:

❏ ❏ ❏ ❏ ❏ ❏ ❏ ❏ ❏ ❏ ❏ ❏ ❏ ❏ ❏ ❏

Signature .... Expiry date ....

Further *Successful Business in a Week* **titles from Hodder & Stoughton and the Institute of Management all at £6.99**

0 340 71205 8	Appraisals in a Week	❏	0 340 71202 3	Leadership in a Week	❏
0 340 70546 9	Assertiveness in a Week	❏	0 340 71173 6	Management Gurus in a Week	❏
0 340 78004 5	Balanced Scorecard in a Week	❏	0 340 78096 7	Managing Your Boss in a Week	❏
0 340 71197 3	Benchmarking in a Week	❏	0 340 74757 9	Marketing in a Week	❏
0 340 78176 9	Body Language in a Week	❏	0 340 47579 7	Marketing Plans in a Week	❏
0 340 57640 5	Budgeting in a Week	❏	0 340 60894 3	Meetings in a Week	❏
0 340 74751 X	Bullying at Work in a Week	❏	0 340 74241 0	Memory Techniques in a Week	❏
0 340 72077 8	Business Growth in a Week	❏	0 340 61137 5	Mentoring in a Week	❏
0 340 70540 X	Business on the Internet in a Week	❏	0 340 71174 4	Mind Maps® in a Week	❏
0 340 71199 X	Business Plans in a Week	❏	0 340 73761 1	Motivation in a Week	❏
0 340 59813 1	Business Writing in a Week	❏	0 340 70545 0	Negotiating in a Week	❏
0 340 62032 3	Computing for Business in a Week	❏	0 340 71123 X	Neuro-Linguistic Programming in a Week	❏
0 340 73781 6	Consultancy in a Week	❏			
0 340 74752 8	Credit Control in a Week	❏	0 340 73812 X	Office Feng Shui in a Week	❏
0 340 71196 5	Customer Care in a Week	❏	0 340 70541 8	Planning Your Own Career in a Week	❏
0 340 70543 4	CVs in a Week	❏			
0 340 75815 5	Cyberm@rketing in a Week	❏	0 340 70544 2	Presentation in a Week	❏
0 340 72076 X	Dealing with Difficult People in a Week	❏	0 340 71208 2	Process Management in a Week	❏
			0 340 70539 6	Project Management in a Week	❏
0 340 78092 4	Dealing with Your Dismissal in a Week	❏	0 340 73780 8	Psychometric Testing in a Week	❏
			0 340 71206 6	Purchasing in a Week	❏
0 340 73762 X	Delegation in a Week	❏	0 340 73816 2	Recruitment in a Week	❏
0 340 62741 7	Direct Mail in a Week	❏	0 340 71198 1	Report Writing in a Week	❏
0 340 75336 6	E-commerce in a Week	❏	0 340 70538 8	Selling in a Week	❏
0 340 73048 X	E-mail in a Week	❏	0 340 77998 5	Speed Reading in a Week	❏
0 340 64330 7	Empowerment in a Week	❏	0 340 72494 3	Strategy in a Week	❏
0 340 77479 7	Facilitation in a Week	❏	0 340 71201 5	Stress Management in a Week	❏
0 340 71192 2	Finance for Non-Financial Managers in a Week	❏	0 340 70542 6	Succeeding at Interviews in a Week	❏
			0 340 71207 4	Teambuilding in a Week	❏
0 340 71189 2	Flexible Working in a Week	❏	0 340 70547 7	Time Management in a Week	❏
0 340 67925 5	Fundraising and Sponsorship in a Week	❏	0 340 71191 4	Total Quality Management in a Week	❏
0 340 71204 X	Going Freelance in a Week	❏	0 340 75785 X	Tough Interview Questions in a Week	❏
0 340 78093 2	Image in a Week	❏			
0 340 74287 9	Information Overload in a Week	❏	0 340 71195 7	Training in a Week	❏
0 340 74756 0	Interviewing in a Week	❏	0 340 70508 6	Web Sites in a Week	❏
0 340 71203 i	Introduction to Bookkeeping and Accounting in a Week	❏	0 340 772552	Winning People Round to Change in a Week	❏
0 340 75337 4	Investors in People in a Week	❏	0 340 78240 4	Writing Great Business Letters in a Week	❏
0 340 75786 8	Knowledge Management in a Week	❏			

All Hodder & Stoughton books are available from your local bookshop or can be ordered direct from the publisher. Just tick the titles you want and fill in the form below. Prices and availability subject to change without notice.

To: Hodder & Stoughton Ltd, Cash Sales Department, Bookpoint, 39 Milton Park, Abingdon, Oxon, OX14 4TD. If you have a credit card you may order by telephone – 01235 400414.

E-mail address: orders@bookpoint.co.uk

Please enclose a cheque or postal order made payable to Bookpoint Ltd to the value of the cover price and allow the following for postage and packaging:

UK & BFPO: £4.30 for one book; £6.30 for two books; £8.30 for three books.

OVERSEAS & EIRE: £4.80 for one book; £7.10 for 2 or 3 books (surface mail).

Name: ....

Address: ....

....

If you would prefer to pay by credit card, please complete:

Please debit my Visa/Mastercard/Diner's Card/American Express (delete as appropriate) card no:

❏ ❏ ❏ ❏ ❏ ❏ ❏ ❏ ❏ ❏ ❏ ❏ ❏ ❏ ❏ ❏

Signature .... Expiry Date ....